RIPPLES OF
WISDOM

CULTIVATING the HIDDEN TRUTHS
FROM YOUR HEART

RIPPLES OF WISDOM

don Jose Ruiz

with Tami Hudman

PLAIN SIGHT PUBLISHING
CEDAR FORT, INC. SPRINGVILLE, UTAH

Library of Congress Cataloging-in-Publication Data on file

ISBN 13: 978-1-4621-1228-9

Published by Plain Sight Publishing, an imprint of Cedar Fort, Inc.
2373 W. 700 S., Springville, UT 84663
Distributed by Cedar Fort, Inc., www.cedarfort.com

Cover and page design by Angela D. Olsen
Cover design © 2013 by Lyle Mortimer
Edited by Whitney A. Lindsley

Printed in China

10 9 8 7 6 5 4 3 2 1

WHEN YOU ARE FEELING fear, limitations, conflict, or drama, you are hearing lies. Whether these lies are coming from something outside of you or from your own thoughts, be aware of them. The truth guides you to peace, happiness, and change. Integrity will always direct you toward love and fulfillment.

YOU ARE THE KING OR QUEEN of your own kingdom. Your kingdom resides in your palace—your physical body. Your palace has a strong vessel inside that gives it, and you, life twenty-four hours a day. Your heart works hard every day without fail. That's why you're alive. Return the favor and take care of your kingdom; take care of your palace. Be aware of what you are putting into your body and your mind. Be aware of your thoughts and actions, and take care of the vessel that is the gift of life.

THE ANGEL OF LIFE COMES into your dream each day and gives you a message, aware or unaware, intentionally or unintentionally. It is talking to you, and you are listening. What message are you allowing life to feed you? Be the filter of your dream. Filter out what is negative, with no judgment. Then learn, listen, and feed your dream with positivity.

THE LANGUAGE OF DO-RE-MI is such a wonderful way to think. When your head is full of inspiring music, it distracts the mind. When the mind is out of the way, you can have pure intent. Music is the language of the Artist; it gets you out of the big mitote in your head.

A LIBRARIAN GOES INTO HER library and opens any story she wants to read or experience. She knows it is just a story, just a book written by someone else being perceived by her. You are your own librarian, and your library is life. You open stories each moment and perceive them in your own way. Be aware of your perception and the stories you are opening. Are they negative or positive? Are they creating peace and love or suffering and pain?

WHEN LIFE SPEAKS TO US through truth, it is guiding us toward our individual, unique nature. The truth is so easy to follow when we are children. When it is overpowered by knowledge, thoughts, and ego, it becomes nearly inaudible. With awareness, truth becomes a whisper; with attention, it becomes audible. Again it is able to guide us back to our truth—knowledge laced with wisdom.

WE ARE IN A WAR WITHIN our own minds. It is a war between our truth and all the opinions and judgments that have been thrown at us or that we have thrown at ourselves. Become a warrior and fight against the parasite in your own mind. Stop being the scorpion that stings itself with its own tail and be skeptical of what you are telling yourself. Listen carefully and allow only the positive to rule and reign, bringing heaven into your existence.

IN ORDER TO SEE YOUR CREATION, to see your truth, you must first let go of everything that is not truth, everything that is a superstition or a lie. Find the courage to let go of what you are not and detach from your story. You will find the truth is so much better than the lies you tell yourself.

THE WORD IS A FORCE THAT you cannot see; however, you can see what this force manifests. The word can create negativity or positivity depending on how you perceive it. It can also create a big story in your mind that isn't truth. Be aware of the words you are letting in and learn to filter those that create negativity in your life.

WHAT IS YOUR IMAGE OF perfection? Where did you acquire that image? *Image* is the important word here. Because that's exactly what it is, an image, an optical illusion. YOU ARE PERFECT. There is nothing to live up to. Accept yourself just how you are today. If YOU want to make a change, TAKE ACTION! But don't take action to live up to someone else's expectations. Take action for yourself. That's the best way to succeed!

Become immune to gossip. When another person uses gossip to communicate, he or she is living in hell by attempting to hurt others. If someone is using gossip to hurt you, remember: If you don't judge yourself, no one else can judge you, and the judgments die in your mind. When you feel comfortable in your truth and are spending your time and energy on yourself, there is no room for gossip. You are too busy creating your own heaven.

WHAT IS TRUTH? IT IS THE force that brings life, love, light, and beauty—the force that opens and closes each flower, that changes the colors of the leaves on the trees. It lives in every being. The truth just is, with no explanation. A lie will lead to fear, limitation, conflict, and drama. Why believe lies? The truth is what is real.

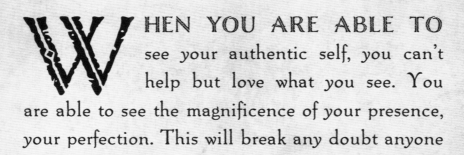

WHEN YOU ARE ABLE TO see your authentic self, you can't help but love what you see. You are able to see the magnificence of your presence, your perfection. This will break any doubt anyone else ever put into your head.

STOP LETTING LIES RULE YOUR world. When you follow your heart, you begin to see the truth. The truth is simple because it simply is, and it survives. The truth doesn't need you to believe in it. When you stop believing in a lie, it disappears. A lie cannot survive your skepticism. Just as a great Master once said, the truth will set you free.

EVERYONE HAS THE RIGHT TO believe what they want to believe. They have the right to feel what they feel and to say what they want to say. If you take everything personally, you may feel defensive or hurt. Instead of judging what others say, listen and show respect. Remember, everything isn't always about you.

RESPECT IS SUCH A BEAUTIFUL offering of love. It is one of the most important symbols we can understand. Respect begins with ourselves. If we don't respect ourselves, it's impossible to respect anyone or anything around us.

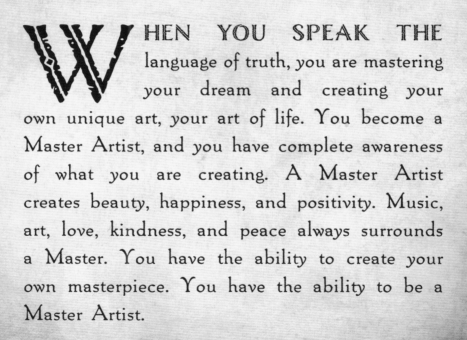

WHEN YOU SPEAK THE language of truth, you are mastering your dream and creating your own unique art, your art of life. You become a Master Artist, and you have complete awareness of what you are creating. A Master Artist creates beauty, happiness, and positivity. Music, art, love, kindness, and peace always surrounds a Master. You have the ability to create your own masterpiece. You have the ability to be a Master Artist.

Have faith in yourself. When you are able to trust yourself completely, you will have no doubt where your power comes from. It comes from you, from the infinite that is you. When you have faith and trust in yourself, your trust in others will come naturally because it won't matter anymore what others say or do.

THE FIRST RULE OF THE ART of happiness is that we are not happy all the time. As humans, we feel emotions. With this awareness, when we feel unhappy, we have the ability to let the uncomfortable emotions move through us and bring us to a place of peace.

EVERY WORD I TELL MYSELF or others is just a symbol that isn't real. These symbols are only made up in my mind and they are my creation, my art. I am the one who gives meaning and power to every piece of artwork I create. When I create a thought in my mind and then give it meaning, it creates a feeling or an emotion within me. With this awareness, I can control the elements within myself. I can be skeptical of what I'm telling myself and make happiness my reality.

THE PRESENCE OF THE INFINITE is everywhere. It is in every flower, every creature, every breath of air, and, most important, it is in you. It is you. Why search for something outside yourself when it is right inside you? When you are living in hell, living in all of your knowledge, or living in darkness, you are unable to see the light that resides within every living being, including you. You are the warmth and the light. You are perfect.

UNCONDITIONALLY LOVE YOUR beloved and your loved ones—the people you say you love the most. Show them the pure love and acceptance of the divine. Enjoy watching them live their lives, living in love without judgment. Allow them to learn, be, and change with no expectations. Bring heaven to yourself and those around you, with the divinity of pure love.

LIVING ON THE ISLAND OF safety is being stuck in a destructive habit, addiction, or cycle that feels so natural, so comfortable. When you step into the sea of creation, you begin to feel the discomfort. Your ego does its best to take hold and pull you back to the island. Allow the uncomfortable feelings to rise and fall like the waves. Instead of allowing them to crash upon you, ride them to the point of creation and find your heaven.

YOU HAVE THE RIGHT TO believe whatever you want to believe, and others have that same right. If we all show respect and listen to others' beliefs and points of view with no judgment, peace would resonate. No more hatred, jealousy, or negativity would exist, and positivity would radiate the earth like the warmth of the sun.

ON'T CONCERN YOURSELF with others' opinions. Others' opinions have absolutely nothing to do with you. With this awareness, you become free. What people think of you is only their own perception of you, a story they have created in their own minds about you. The real you is beyond everything you know, and, most definitely, beyond what others think they know of you.

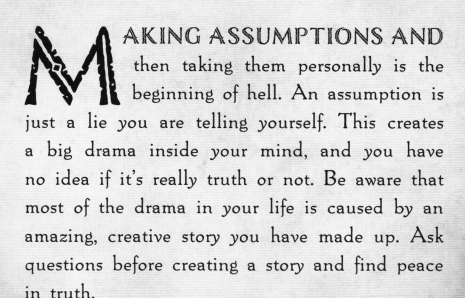

MAKING ASSUMPTIONS AND then taking them personally is the beginning of hell. An assumption is just a lie you are telling yourself. This creates a big drama inside your mind, and you have no idea if it's really truth or not. Be aware that most of the drama in your life is caused by an amazing, creative story you have made up. Ask questions before creating a story and find peace in truth.

IF YOU MAKE A CHANGE IN yourself, you will change the world. When you love yourself, enjoy life, and make your personal world a dream of heaven, just like magic, the world around you begins to change. You find the reality that changing another person is not possible, but changing your own actions, reactions, and perceptions can bring a change to everything in the world surrounding you.

BE IN COMPLETE POWER OF your own creation. Words are the seeds of the creation of life. Be the gardener of your life, and plant your seeds with love and integrity. To honor yourself is to have responsibility of your garden.

ACCEPTANCE IS THE WAY TO live without judgment. If you accept yourself and allow yourself to be as you are, there will be no self-judgment. If you accept others just as they are, any judgment you have against another will diminish. This allows you to remove all conflict with yourself and others. Then something incredible happens: you find peace.

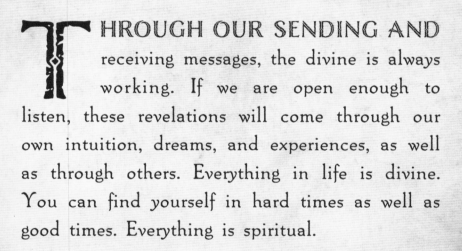

THROUGH OUR SENDING AND receiving messages, the divine is always working. If we are open enough to listen, these revelations will come through our own intuition, dreams, and experiences, as well as through others. Everything in life is divine. You can find yourself in hard times as well as good times. Everything is spiritual.

KNOW THAT YOU ARE DREAMING and perceiving the dream of the divine— the divine enjoying its creation, awakening in you. When you close your eyes, you connect with the divine without separation. You open your first instinct of being, your truth—love. This is the reason we are all one.

EVERYONE HAS THEIR OWN language, their own perception of life, including what creates happiness. With awareness, when you step into a world of advice or self-help, take only the gems and the words of love that speak to you. Take your power back from your own dream. That is your language.

NOBODY CAN WRITE YOUR story for you, and you cannot write another person's story. Respect is allowing others to have their dreams, to allow them to create freely. When others are telling you how to dress, how to walk, how to talk, or how to live your life, they are not respecting your story. When you try to control another person's story, all your energy goes to negativity, and you lose your freedom.

IMAGINE THE UNION BETWEEN you and your body if you were completely loyal to your body, if you were completely grateful for your body, and if you treated your body with justice. Imagine how different your life would be if you lived with gratitude, love, loyalty, and justice, beginning with yourself.

WHEN YOU RESPECT AND love yourself, you can be in a happy relationship with another person who respects and loves himself or herself. This creates a beautiful interaction of unconditional love. What you offer is what you receive.

THE CREATOR, THE TOLTEC, the Artist, YOU are perceiving your dream with awareness. YOU are taking responsibility for your creation and using your canvas as a tool to create your heaven. YOU are attaching and detaching to every breath, every gift of life that flows through you. Moving away from the lies created by the words and symbols of others and your own mind, you become aware of the divine truth, the Creator, the Toltec, the Artist, YOU.

WHEN WE BEGIN TO DREAM that we are not God, that is when the nightmare begins. We fall from heaven and land in hell. We begin to search for God, and we begin to search for ourselves. The knowledge we have attained and the beliefs from other humans of what they think we are take over. These beliefs distort the truth of what we really are: a reflection of God, the truth that I AM.

RESPECT YOUR HUMANITY. Put all the awareness into that gift that was given to you by the Creator. If you are enjoying yourself, doing what you love with happiness and peace, then you are taking care of your gift. When you feel the butterflies of fear or pain creep in, it is time to take action. Pick yourself up and carry yourself through the pain or fear, finding the love and peace, to create a beautiful heaven.

THE HIGHEST POINT OF YOUR journey back to your authentic self is when you see the magnificence of your presence and how wonderful and beautiful you truly are. You see your own perfection, and you become aware that you are light, you are life, you are your own divinity, and your reflection becomes clear.

A LOVER OF DREAMS IS ONE who accepts and allows others to dream their dreams, to be themselves with no judgments or opinions. A lover of dreams feeds the flame of life with the kindling of love and acceptance. A lover of dreams lives each moment in the point of creation, taking action, manifesting a love for life.

LEARN TO LISTEN. WHEN YOU learn to listen, you begin to understand the meaning of the symbols that others are using. You begin to understand their story, and communication and clarity between you and others will begin to improve.

IMAGINE LIVING WITHOUT FEAR, without judgment. Imagine being yourself, and not trying to convince anybody of anything. Imagine that wherever you go, heaven is going with you. Imagine living with complete freedom. Yes, the truth will set you free, but first you need to see the truth. Find your personal truth and take heaven wherever you go.

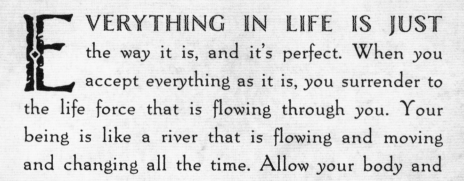

EVERYTHING IN LIFE IS JUST the way it is, and it's perfect. When you accept everything as it is, you surrender to the life force that is flowing through you. Your being is like a river that is flowing and moving and changing all the time. Allow your body and your mind to flow freely and enjoy just being.

To FEEL INSPIRATION AND see beyond knowledge, opinions, and judgments is to surrender to love, to live in every moment, to detach and let go. Unconditional love for life brings the awareness of infinity and expands the unity and gratitude of all as ONE.

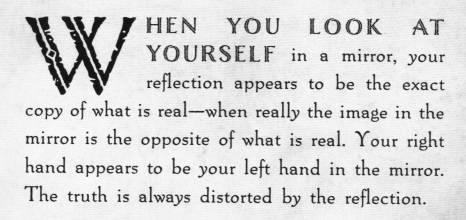

WHEN YOU LOOK AT YOURSELF in a mirror, your reflection appears to be the exact copy of what is real—when really the image in the mirror is the opposite of what is real. Your right hand appears to be your left hand in the mirror. The truth is always distorted by the reflection.

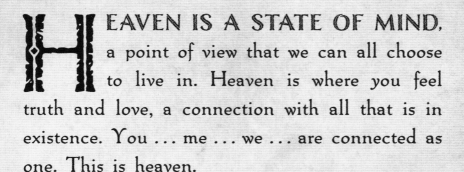

HEAVEN IS A STATE OF MIND, a point of view that we can all choose to live in. Heaven is where you feel truth and love, a connection with all that is in existence. You . . . me . . . we . . . are connected as one. This is heaven.

WHEN YOU STAND IN THE river against the current, disappointed in what the river took away, you are stagnant to all the beautiful things that are flowing around you today. When you flow with the river, you are flowing with life. Imagine what you will catch if you are riding the current, flowing with awareness.

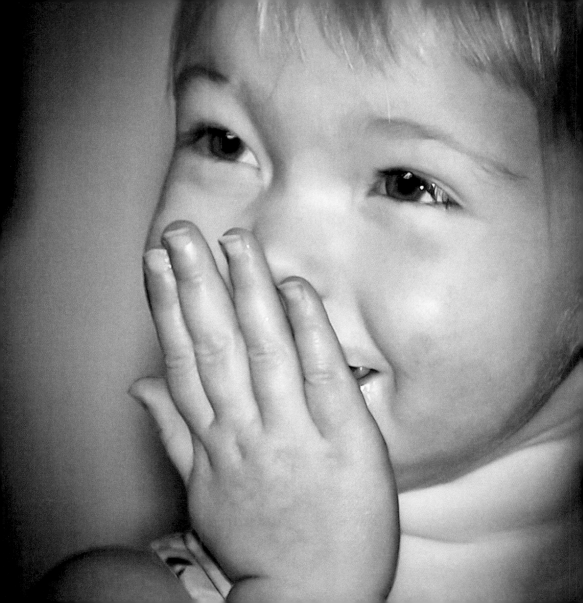

YOU DON'T HAVE TO SEARCH for heaven; heaven is in you. You don't have to search for happiness; happiness is in you. You don't have to search for the truth; you are the truth. You don't have to search for love; you are love. Be the real you, your authentic self. Now that's wisdom.

WHEN YOU LOVE YOURSELF unconditionally, you are not afraid to express your love. You live your life in love and see that love reflected in everyone around you. Love is your truth, your nature. See love come out of you like the light from the sun.

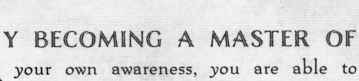

BY BECOMING A MASTER OF your own awareness, you are able to control your choices and master the dream of your life. With this wisdom, along with intent and action, you can create anything you wish. So why not use your imagination and create your deepest desires?

ESPECTING OTHERS BRINGS peace into your life. Allowing others to have their own beliefs, to live the life they choose, without any disrespect or judgment, means you are not in conflict with anyone. You are living in peace.

WHEN YOU ARE READY TO make a change in your life, when you are ready to change your agreements, the most important thing is awareness. What agreements do you need to make with yourself and those around you to create the life you desire? Then practice by taking action. Awareness + Action = Change.

YOU HAVE THE OPPORTUNITY each day to begin a new creation. Your canvas is blank when you awake in the morning. Before the words begin to flow in your mind, stop them and enjoy the beauty of the silence, the white space, the space in between. That space is where creation begins. Then, with awareness, positivity, and action, start creating a beautiful piece of art.